SCUNTHORPE
IN OLD PHOTOGRAPHS

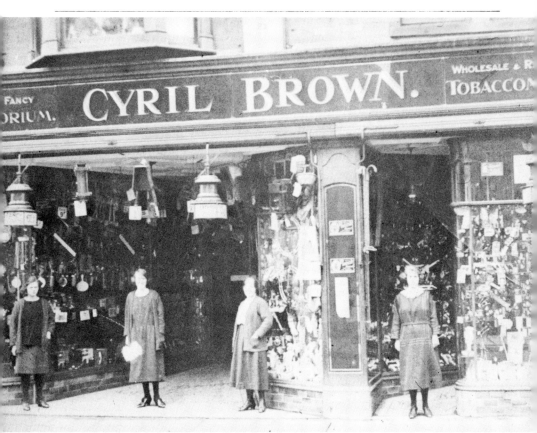

CYRIL BROWN'S TOBACCONIST and Fancy Goods Emporium at 59 and 59A High Street in the early 1930s. Products as diverse as umbrellas, walking sticks, dressing cases, pocket wallets, smokers' requisites, rocking horses, dolls' prams, Meccano and croquet sets could be purchased here.

SCUNTHORPE
IN OLD PHOTOGRAPHS

COMPILED BY
DAVID TAYLOR

ALAN SUTTON
Scunthorpe Museums

Alan Sutton Publishing Limited
Phoenix Mill · Far Thrupp · Stroud · Gloucestershire

First published 1991

British Library Cataloguing in Publication Data

Scunthorpe in old photographs.
I. Taylor, David
942.831

ISBN 0-7509-0002-4

Typeset in 9/10 Korinna.
Typesetting and origination by
Alan Sutton Publishing Limited.
Printed in Great Britain by
The Bath Press, Avon.

CONTENTS

ROAD MENDING IN STATION ROAD around 1920. The hoardings on the left are advertising Holder Brothers' music shop on the High Street and programmes at the Empire Theatre. The blast furnaces of Frodingham Iron and Steel Co. loom in the background.

FOREWORD

Most of the development of Scunthorpe has taken place within living memory of our residents who, like myself, will experience deep feelings of nostalgia as they view these old photographs and recall how our town used to look. There is also a keen interest among younger generations to see the conditions under which their parents and grandparents lived, worked and played and they too will derive great enjoyment from seeing their town as it was.

Development of the steelworks was the main driving force behind Scunthorpe's expansion which saw the population double in the forty years from 1931 to 1971. My grandparents brought their family from Holland to Scunthorpe in 1907 so that my grandfather could find work in the steelworks. At one time they lived in Trafford Street (close to St John's Church) and then obtained a house to rent in Laneham Street. However, after a little while my grandmother decided she could not settle there as she was lonely and 'too far away from her friends' in Trafford Street! Such an attitude seems incomprehensible now, but it was very real in those early days of the century.

I suppose it says a lot for our resilience when we contemplate the changes that have taken place and the way we have coped, particularly in these latter years. In this computerized age and at a time when engines perform wonderful feats and are rated in thousands of horsepower, I can sit back and recall seeing bread vans and grocery carts trundling through our streets, each drawn by one horse. I can still picture the two-horse troughs which served to quench their thirst – one outside where Woolworths is and the other outside St John's Church. Or, as we marvel at how goods and services are paid for with credit cards and automatic deductions from bank accounts, I remember waiting in the local Co-op for my change to come back from the cash desk in a little container that zoomed along a wire. That seemed just as remarkable as what happens today.

We cannot stop change and indeed if we want to develop then there have to be changes. We should realize, however, that change is not always beneficial and an understanding of the past can help us to change for the better. These photographs show Scunthorpe when it was five separate villages each with its own community, ideas and interests. We have learned to come together and to live and work as one town for our mutual benefit. That is an achievement that could be followed with advantage nationally and internationally.

I am proud to have been born in Scunthorpe, to have lived here all my life and to have helped in the development of our town. I am honoured and delighted to make my small contribution towards the production of this book. I shall derive great pleasure looking at the photographs and I hope that you do too.

Councillor Oliver Duffelen
Chairman, Scunthorpe Leisure Services Committee

INTRODUCTION

This volume consists of a selection of photographs, drawn mainly from the collections of Scunthorpe Museum and Art Gallery, that depict aspects of life in Scunthorpe over the last hundred years or so. Very few have been published before. Inevitably the selection may not appear entirely representative, but nevertheless the broad intention has been to try to create something of the flavour of the town's past from the second half of the last century up to 1970. The latter date has been chosen as the cut-off point because, with the building of the new pedestrianized shopping precinct and the demolition of local landmarks, such as the Blue Bell Hotel, what many regarded as 'old Scunthorpe' seemed to have disappeared overnight.

However, *Scunthorpe in Old Photographs* does not pretend to be a comprehensive history of the town; that has been successfully achieved elsewhere. Rather, it is hoped that it will complement existing works, and perhaps also highlight a few of the more esoteric highways and byways of Scunthorpe's history.

Scunthorpe is a relatively new town, and it has become something of a cliché to describe it as having developed rapidly from five small agricultural villages after iron was first manufactured in the area in 1864. Nevertheless, the census returns bear this out; from a combined population of 1,413 in 1861, the number of people living in the area had grown to 11,167 inside forty years, and the figures continued to rise.

From the photographic point of view, this has meant that although there are fewer nineteenth-century photographs than have been taken in more established communities, the town is still well represented by the postcard boom that took place before the First World War. There were several professional photographers working in Scunthorpe at that time, of whom the most notable was Arthur Henry Singleton who deserves more than just local recognition.

Old photographs are now more readily accessible than ever before, and a source of great enjoyment in the almost magical way they can recapture memories of time and place. It is thus possible to underestimate their value as historical documents. The camera rarely lies and it has the ability to record the past in a way that often supersedes that of the written and recorded spoken word. Despite this, old photographs do need to be treated with some circumspection; many of the examples in this book were obviously arranged to show their subjects in the best possible light, not in their everyday lives.

We view old photographs with the benefit of an often considerable degree of hindsight. We see buildings that have since been demolished, streets that are no longer recognizable, and people we once knew as children. We also see customs, activities and ways of living that have now disappeared in the name of progress and social change. Looking back can be instructive as well as enjoyable and it is hoped that reading this compilation will be both.

SECTION ONE

Ashby

A PEACEFUL SCENE IN ASHBY HIGH STREET taken after the construction of the Crown Hotel on the left in 1909 by Fox's Brewery of Crowle. It replaced an earlier 'Crown' on the same site and at the time was the largest hotel in the district. Without today's heavy traffic, children could play safely on the street.

THIS PHOTOGRAPH IS SIMILAR TO THE ONE ABOVE except that it was taken some twenty years later in the 1930s, and from slightly further to the west. Apart from the appearance of telegraph poles, not much else has changed. Two of the three buildings in front of the Crown Hotel survive today.

BOTTESFORD LANE, ASHBY, looking towards the High Street around 1905 when there were only houses on the left-hand side of the Lane. It was re-named Bottesford Road soon after this photograph was taken.

KENDALL MEMORIAL PRIMITIVE METHODIST CHAPEL, with its schoolroom which was built in 1885 on the site of present-day Ashby Market. The chapel was named after Thomas Kendall, a Primitive Methodist preacher and other members of his large family; six of his sons also became preachers (although not all Primitive Methodists). It was demolished in 1962, and not surprisingly the name of the road in front was Chapel Street.

ST PAUL'S CHURCH, ASHBY, the original 'Tin Tabernacle', seen from the High Street. An early prefabricated building constructed in corrugated iron, it was opened on the site of the present church on 26 January 1899. The turret contained a single bell.

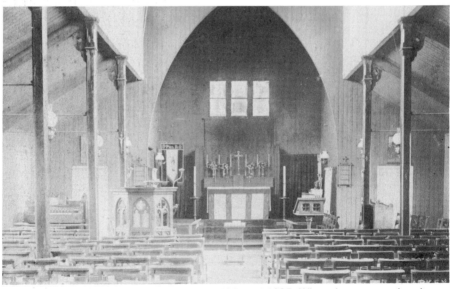

INTERIOR OF THE 'TIN TABERNACLE', between 1899 and 1925. When the present church was opened, this temporary building was retained as a church hall. Couples needed great skill in order to avoid bumping into the pillars during dances! It finally disappeared in 1939, when a new, purpose-built hall was erected.

SCENE FROM A NATIVITY PLAY taken in St Paul's Church Hall. All the actors appear to be adults.

KIRTON TERRACE decorated for the coronation of George V. The road in front was known as the 'Screeds' and ended at a kissing gate on the parish boundary between Ashby and Brumby. From there a footpath led north to Scunthorpe High Street. The terrace, which also became known as the 'Screeds', was built in 1885, and finally demolished in the 1960s. The word means a narrow strip of land. Another Ashby name of some antiquity was the 'Smootings'. This described a passageway that once linked Ashby High Street with the Screeds.

A CROWD OF CHILDREN POSE for the camera outside a grocer's shop on Ashby High Street. Like many of the photographs in this book, it dates from the years immediately preceding the First World War. The two shops which adjoin the Brown Cow public house survive virtually unchanged today; the one on the right was for many years Elsie's newsagents.

THE STAFF AND RATHER AUSTERE EXTERIOR of Scunthorpe Co-operative Society's Ashby Branch taken in February 1904. Opened on the lower part of High Street on 10 October 1896, this was the Society's number two branch. A public tea was held in Ashby Junior School to mark the occasion of its opening, and the first week's takings were £25. At this time, Co-operative stores were cheaper and provided a wider choice than the average corner shop and, in addition, the quarterly dividend paid to the customers was often a welcome bonus.

CROWDS GATHERED at the opening of Ashby Library on 16 April 1906. Standing next to the lady in the wide-brimmed hat is the first librarian Mr Clement Kendall who remained in the post until his death in 1931. In his obituary he was described as 'certainly the best known man in Ashby'. Among his many achievements he was a founder member and secretary of Ashby Institute, and the first man in Ashby to own a pneumatically tyred bicycle, described as a 'fearful and wonderful sight'. The haystack on the right of the photograph belonged to one of the farms still working on Ashby High Street at this time.

ASHBY HIGH STREET looking east around 1910. On the left, behind the two children on the pavement, is the entrance to Ashby Junior School. Opened in 1881, it was the second oldest school in Scunthorpe until its closure in 1988.

NATHAN BILTON'S BAKERY in Ashby High Street around 1910. Both this building and its neighbour, with their distinctive decorated gabled roofs, are still shops today. They are situated opposite Appleton Way which for many years was known as 'Queen Street'. Mr Bilton was keen to advertise his business; at one time his name was even painted on the roof.

MANOR FARMHOUSE, ASHBY, taken shortly before it was demolished in the early 1950s. This handsome building which once stood on the site of Manor Park on Burringham Road was the fulcrum of a large farm.

A HORSE-DRAWN SCUNTHORPE CO-OPERATIVE SOCIETY BREAD VAN snapped in Priory Lane around 1951. Peggy Smith is on the left with Rose Waterfall, and their horse 'Bowler'. These vehicles were once a common sight in Scunthorpe until they were withdrawn not long after this photograph was taken. They delivered bread and cakes several times a week to houses in Scunthorpe and surrounding villages, as well as supplying outlying Co-operative branches.

RECENTLY CONSTRUCTED COUNCIL HOUSES on the Riddings Estate in 1957. Dad digs the new garden as mum and Rover look on.

A TEAM OF POTATO PICKERS from Ashby at the turn of the century. This traditional seasonal activity has ended only very recently.

SECTION TWO

Brumby

A DONKEY-POWERED LAWN-MOWER being used to cut the lawn outside the entrance to Brumby Hall in the 1920s. The groundsman is Tommy Sanderson, who was employed by Appleby-Frodingham Athletic Club Committee until his retirement in 1936, and the donkey was known as 'Lammy's donkey' after one of his assistants Lammy Nichols. At first the groundsman relied on a single animal shod with leather boots to do the heavy mowing and rolling, but this was later increased to two, which were eventually superseded by a horse. Tommy's first working experience on the estate was as a labourer at the tender age of eleven when he was paid 7d. a day. He was legendary among the sporting fraternity, and died in 1960, aged 89.

CROWDS GATHERED TO WATCH a pre-First World War monoplane in the grounds of Brumby Hall. It was flown by an aviator called Marcus Manton, who during an aerobatic display became the first man to 'loop the loop' over Scunthorpe.

A SCENE BARELY RECOGNIZABLE TODAY; this view looking south down Ashby Road was taken by James Henderson around 1900. On the right is an entrance leading into the grounds of Brumby Hall.

NO. 61 OLD BRUMBY STREET taken in the 1920s. Still extant today, the cottage dates, however, from the mid-nineteenth century, and reminds us of Brumby's rural past. Constructed in whitewashed, roughly coursed ironstone with a pantile roof, it has been designated a listed building.

OLD BRUMBY STREET in 1905. Today this is one of the few places in Scunthorpe that still retains something of the atmosphere of the town's pre-industrial past. The village pinfold where cattle were once impounded stood in front of the house in the centre.

LOCAL CHILDREN PICTURED outside 16 Old Brumby Street in 1931. Most of them are dressed for winter weather. Among the group are Ken Stebbins, Jack Ancliff, Elsie Belton, Joyce Bath, Arthur Childs, Herbert Belton, Arthur Holloway, Barbara Larwood, Marjorie Larwood, Betty Clixby, Merle Clixby, Dorothy Cabourn, Cliff Atkinson, Jeff Atkinson, Vincent Slack, Bert Smith, Ray Simpson, Dan Larwood, Sid Allen, Hubert Jakes, Kenny Winter, Vernon Williams and Peter Thompson.

A TRANQUIL OLD BRUMBY STREET looking north around 1910. The gable end of the building furthest from the camera belongs to a former farmhouse which is still standing.

THIS ATTRACTIVE FARMHOUSE AT 27 OLD BRUMBY STREET, which originally dates from around 1790, is here seen early this century when it was rebuilt and enlarged. Behind it are various cowsheds, stables and other farm buildings of similar antiquity.

KISSING GATE AND FOOTPATH, Brumby, in 1905.

CHAPEL STREET, NEW BRUMBY, taken sometime around 1910, looking towards Cottage Beck Road. The shops on the left are Powell King's cycle repairers and a hairdressers. New Brumby was a similar industrial community to New Frodingham, centred around Beauchamp, Chapel and Lygon Streets. It was built by the Beauchamp family in the 1880s and faced the older community of New Frodingham across Cottage Beck Road (which marked the boundary between the two parishes). At this time, New Brumby seems to have been something of a shopping centre, with twenty shops listed in Kelly's Directory, far more than its neighbour.

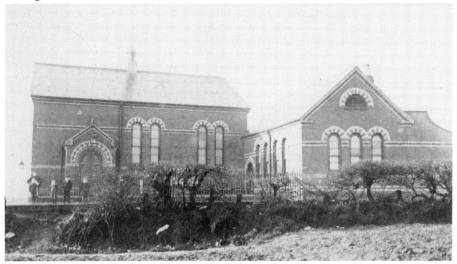

A PRIMITIVE METHODIST CHAPEL that once stood on the corner of Chapel Street and Cottage Beck Road, photographed from some allotments opposite. It was constructed in 1877 with the schoolroom on the right added in 1892. The present Methodist church on Cottage Beck Road was erected on the same site in 1965.

SECTION THREE

Crosby

FRODINGHAM ROAD looking north in 1927. Porter Street is on the right opposite the Centenary Methodist Primitive Chapel opened by Lady Sheffield on 12 October 1908. The chapel was almost entirely destroyed by fire in 1970. Delivery boys on trade cycles were a common sight in the streets between the wars when goods, particularly meat and groceries, were transported to the home.

SCUNTHORPE AND DISTRICT WORKINGMEN'S CLUB and Institute and the Crosby Hotel in 1911. When this photograph was taken, both these buildings had been recently constructed, the Institute from a collection made by steelworkers. It was also known as the 'Big Social', having previously had premises in Cross Street, and for many years was the leading workingmen's club in Scunthorpe. In the early days, the huge basement was fitted with baths and showers. The premises are now occupied by JJ's nightclub.

SCUNTHORPE BIG SOCIAL CLUB'S Old Age Pensioners' Club Committee in the early 1930s.

A FISHING TRIP ORGANIZED by the Crosby Workingmen's Club ready to set off from outside the Crosby Hotel in 1911. The vehicles were hired from Henry Skelton and Son; the one in front is a wagonette, followed by a trap for the club's officials.

STAFF OF THE CROSBY HOTEL taken soon after it was built by the People's Refreshment Association in 1910 in an attractive Edwardian arts-and-crafts style. A price list from 1911 lists Scotch whisky at 4d. a gill, and ale, stout, cider, dry ginger and minerals at 3d. The hotel was run for many years by the Beck family.

THE PLEASANT TEA GARDEN and bowling green that once stood behind the Crosby Hotel.

A VERY RESIDENTIAL FRODINGHAM ROAD looking north towards Old Crosby in 1927. The cast-iron railings on the garden walls are a feature rarely seen today.

ONE OF THE MANY SHOPS to have traded on Frodingham Road over the years was Donner's Pork Stores at No. 147, between Berkeley Street and Smith Street. It is pictured here in the early 1930s on a postcard complete with a Christmas message. Frodingham Road was originally built as a residential street, hence the front garden of the house next door, but by the 1920s small shops and businesses were beginning to spring up. Today its appearance is that of an old fashioned High Street before the dawning of the age of the supermarket.

CROSBY ELEMENTARY AND INFANTS SCHOOL before 1923, when the distinctive War Memorial was erected in the school playground. The school was opened in 1908, with Mr George Taylor as its first headmaster. The memorial with its delicately carved figure of an angel, commemorates former pupils from the school and the men of Crosby parish who were killed during the First World War.

EMPIRE DAY CELEBRATIONS at Crosby School on 24 May 1910. Rather incongruously, the flag waved by the teacher on the left is a Stars and Stripes. Empire Day was held every year on this date.

CROSBY WORKINGMEN'S CLUB on Frodingham Road decorated for the peace celebrations at the end of the First World War. The premises, which consist of three houses joined together, are now known as the 'Frodingham Road Club'.

INTERIOR OF CROSBY MISSION CHURCH, known as the 'Iron Room', decorated for Easter. It was opened on 28 October 1907, but was not dedicated to St George until 6 December 1913. A new parish church was built on Frodingham Road to replace it and was consecrated on 3 October 1925.

SHEFFIELD STREET taken in the 1920s.

6761A

A TYPICAL TERRACED HOUSE in Crosby of a type known as 'bye-law' housing. The owners, Mr Charles Herbert Bird and his wife Sarah are standing outside, with their son Wilfred. Its address is 12 Sheffield Street. These streets sprang up at the turn of the century, when the majority landowners, the Sheffields, sold much of their land for house building. Consequently many of the street names have Sheffield family connotations.

KEEN BEEKEEPERS IN OLD CROSBY, taken around the turn of the century. The lady is standing behind a traditional type of bee-skep.

LOOKING DOWN OLD CROSBY towards the junction with Frodingham and Ferry Roads in the early 1960s. This was the main street of the old village of Crosby, and some of the cottages from those days still survive. More, alas, have disappeared.

MRS ALICE DENT and child outside her cottage in Old Crosby.

THE VILLAGE BLACKSMITH'S SHOP in Crosby taken before the turn of the century. It was situated just to the north of Old Crosby. The blacksmith, John Ward, can be seen, with his wife and two daughters. Of interest is the handpump in the foreground, the source of their water supply.

CHILDREN PLAYING outside prefabricated houses in Foxhills Road in the 1950s. This was during a decade when Scunthorpe's population was increasing by over a 1,000 inhabitants a year. In all, a total of 800 prefabricated dwellings were built after the Second World War as a short-term remedy for a housing shortage. Some are still in use today.

Frodingham

FRODINGHAM OR 'SCOTTER ROAD' VIADUCT taken from Brumby Wood Lane before the arches were filled in and embanked. The viaduct is 1,020 yd long and consists of 85 arches. In the days of steam locomotives it was said that it served as a useful guide to the weather. If engines coming up it could be clearly heard in Crosby, then it was a sure sign of rain!

A PICTURESQUE VIEW OF BRUMBY WOOD LANE in 1912 looking west down the hill.

BRUMBY WOOD LANE, looking east. The houses on the right date from the 1920s and were built around the time this postcard was published by George Kenning, a stationer of Scunthorpe.

AN ATTRACTIVE VIEW OF ST LAWRENCE'S CHURCH taken around the turn of the century before it was comprehensively rebuilt in 1913. Parts of the church date back to the later twelfth century, making it the oldest surviving building in Scunthorpe. St Lawrence's was reconstructed in 1913, the architect being Sir Charles Nicholson, who designed a new nave, chancel and north aisle. The gravestones were moved to the church's perimeter walls in 1956.

INTERIOR OF ST LAWRENCE'S, also taken before 1913, with the chancel decorated for Easter Sunday. The church's original patron saint was St Mary, and it is thought that the change to its present dedication came about when the living was given to Revesby Abbey in the fifteenth century. With the exception of the tower, the church was extensively rebuilt in 1841 during the great period of Victorian church reconstruction. It was also extended in 1913. Note the oil lamps with which the church was lit at this time.

SCENE TAKEN OUTSIDE ST LAWRENCE'S CHURCH during the consecration of the extensions on Saturday 7 June 1913. Second from the end of the procession is the Bishop of Lincoln, Edward Lee Hicks, who was enthroned in 1910, succeeding Bishop Edward King. He preached to a large congregation, and proposed a vote of thanks to Lord St Oswald (who had contributed £5,000 of the £6,000 cost), and to the architect, the builder and the workmen. The sentence of consecration was read by the vicar of St John's Church, the Revd Thomas Boughton, and a tea was held afterwards in Frodingham School.

A FINE VIEW OF FRODINGHAM VICARAGE, now Scunthorpe Museum & Art Gallery, taken from the south in 1912. It was built in 1875, on the site of Frodingham Hall, the only remains of which are a pair of stone gate pillars. The vicar in 1912 was the Revd Cyprian T. Rust, who was the incumbent until 1947.

MRS GRACE PARROTT (or Miss Hill as she was then known), photographed in her maid's uniform. Between 1928 and 1933 she worked as a parlour maid for Canon and Mrs Rust at Frodingham Vicarage. The Rusts also employed another maid, a cook and a chauffeur/gardener. This photograph was taken in the grounds of Haverholme House in Appleby.

CHURCH LANE at the turn of the century, with the camera pointed towards the crest of the hill.

A VIEW OF THE ROUNDABOUT at the junction of Oswald Road, Church Lane and Station Road in the 1950s. In front of the Central Post Office, opened in 1939, is a horse-drawn Co-operative bread van travelling at speed. These were once a familiar sight in Scunthorpe delivering bread and cakes from the Co-op's bakery in Rowland Road.

THE THATCHED ROOF and whitewashed walls of an old cottage that stood at the corner of Station Road and Oswald Road until it was demolished in 1910. Station Road was known as Water Lane until 1928. The last owner of the cottage was Tommy Balderson, nicknamed 'deaf and dumb Tommy'.

A METICULOUSLY ARRANGED PHOTOGRAPH taken outside Oswald Farm, Frodingham, which stood close to the site of the present railway station. This photograph must date from after the farm was bought by Mr R.I. Swaby, the landlord of the Blue Bell Hotel, and the two boys are his grandsons Bernard and Rowland. The formal nature of the photograph and the best clothes of the boys, suggests it was taken before or after the cattle were shown at an agricultural show.

FRODINGHAM SCHOOL, ROWLAND ROAD, photographed in 1919. Built by the Winn family in 1867, it is Scunthorpe's oldest school. In the year the photograph was taken, the children were given an extra week's holiday to celebrate the signing of the Versailles peace treaty formally ending the First World War.

GIRLS FROM FRODINGHAM SCHOOL dressed for Empire Day during the First World War. After 1904, Empire Day was held on 24 May each year on the anniversary of Queen Victoria's birthday.

ROWLAND ROAD looking west in 1954 with major road works in progress. They were part of a project to lay a water pipeline from the Trent to Redbourn Steelworks. The houses on the left were built as part of the Redbourn village housing scheme. Scunthorpe Co-operative Society's model bakery, completed in 1924, can also be seen on the right.

TRENT STREET, NEW FRODINGHAM, taken from the south before the turn of the century. The entire street seems to have turned out for this photograph. Originally called First Street South, it was renamed after the Trent Ironworks where most of its residents were employed.

CLIFF STREET was another of the New Frodingham terraces built in the 1860s and 1870s. Photographed from the north, the street is shown decorated with a magnificent array of bunting in honour of the coronation of Her Majesty the Queen on 2 June 1953.

THE BAINES FAMILY were long-standing residents of 10 Cliff Street. This is Jack Baines snapped with his nephew Peter Toyne in the 'ten foot' at the rear of the terrace around 1950.

THE LEANING FAMILY in the backyard of 9 Redbourne Street around 1930. Seated from left to right are: Violet Leaning, Frank Leaning and Ernest Leaning. At one time, the inhabitants of Redbourne Street all worked at the Redbourn Hill Iron & Coal Company.

A PIGEON LOFT belonging to local inhabitants on land to the east of Queen Street, New Frodingham in the 1930s. George 'Tinker' Markham of Lindsey Street is on the left and Frank Leaning of Redbourne Street on the right. Racing pigeons was a regular Saturday afternoon pastime. The terrace behind the loft was built after 1907 by the landlord of the Queen Hotel, William Woodley. It was consequently known as 'Woodley's Terrace', although its official name was then Sixth Street North. It was also nicknamed 'railway terrace', because the first inhabitants were employees of the Great Central Railway, and visiting enginemen from other districts often lodged there.

TRENT STREET VICTORY PARTY in 1918 celebrating the signing of the armistice treaty ending the First World War. Separate parties were held for boys and girls on allotments to the north of the street. At the end of the table in the centre are Mr and Mrs Harold Butcher of 11 Trent Street.

Scunthorpe

LOCAL AMATEUR PHOTOGRAPHER Percy Twidale took this photograph from the footbridge of Scunthorpe's second main line station in the mid-1920s. It captures an ex-Great Central Railway, London & North Eastern Railway locomotive entering from the Doncaster direction, with a goods train judging by the lack of passengers.

PASSENGERS WAIT underneath the awnings of the down platform of Frodingham & Scunthorpe station for a train to Grimsby, c. 1905. This was Scunthorpe's second station on the Doncaster–Grimsby line, built in 1887, approximately where Brigg road bridge is today. It closed when the present railway station was opened on 11 March 1928.

A PANORAMIC VIEW across the station goods yard in a photograph taken around 1910 from the top of a blast furnace belonging to Frodingham Iron & Steel Works. Familiar buildings include St John's Church, Scunthorpe windmill, and the old courthouse and police station. Accommodated in the crowded yard are railway wagons from as far afield as the Glasgow & South Western Railway and the London & North Western Railway. Beyond is the single platform terminus of the North Lindsey Light Railway which between 1906 and 1925 provided passenger services to Winterton, West Halton, Winteringham and Whitton.

STATION ROAD (now known as High Street East), c. 1910. In the foreground is Scunthorpe's first library, constructed in 1904, with the former Constitutional Club next door. The road was well named, as there were two railway stations on it at the time.

AN UNUSUAL PHOTOGRAPH taken from the slag banks of the redundant Lindsey Ironworks. It shows the east end of St John's Church, and on the left the rear of the Constitutional Club. In the centre is Dawes Lane, bisected by the North Lindsey Light Railway which was constructed in 1906. This photograph appears to have been taken soon afterwards. Standing at the entrance to the lane are an interesting pair of cottages which for many years have been the offices of the engineering firm of Hornsby & Goodwyn. They were originally constructed in 1886 by the Winn family to the same design as their estate cottages in Appleby.

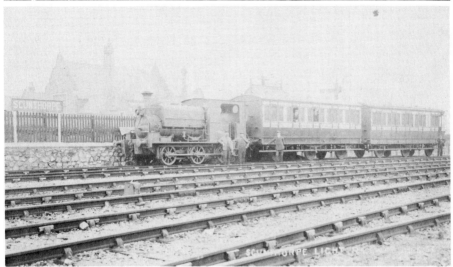

'SCUNTHORPE' STATION on the North Lindsey Light Railway; this single platformed affair was its southern terminus. The 0–6–0 tank locomotive is a contractor's engine called *Bletcher* which was owned by the Doncaster firm of Logan and Hemingway, and built by Manning Wardle of Leeds. The cost of a return ticket from here to West Halton in 1906 was the princely sum of 1s.

AN UNUSUAL VIEW OF SCUNTHORPE WINDMILL which, as the caption suggests, was a four-sail tower mill. Known as 'Long's Mill', it was erected by Uriah Long in 1858, who bought the site from the previous miller, William Wigglesworth. The mill was equipped with an ogee cap, typical of Lincolnshire windmills, a replica of which was fitted in 1982. It survives today as part of the Old Mill public house.

ST JOHN'S CHURCH features in many postcards of old Scunthorpe both as a landmark and because of the excellence of its architecture. This example was taken from the north on a sunny Edwardian afternoon. The church clock, supplied by the Leeds firm of W. Potts & Sons, fixes the time at five minutes to four. Also in view is the small perimeter wall and the north porch.

THE INTERIOR OF ST JOHN'S with the camera pointed towards the chancel. The inside of the church is entirely lined with Ancaster stone and is rather plain compared with its ornate exterior. The exceptions were the richly carved font and pulpit. The pews seated 500 worshippers.

MARKET HILL IN THE 1960s before the shopping precinct development. Kirman's Ironmongers is on the corner with the usual clutter of domestic hardware outside. It was customary to return these items into the shop exactly at closing time, not a minute sooner or later! Next door is the former public library, built in 1899 as a Wesleyan Methodist chapel. It later served as Scunthorpe & Frodingham Urban District Council offices.

A SLEEPY WELLS STREET in 1904; the most striking feature here is the Lord Roberts Hotel built four years earlier. It was named after the well-known soldier, Field Marshal Frederick Roberts, who had successfully commanded British forces in the Boer War. The pub's nickname 'The Lord Bobs' echoes that of its namesake which was 'Bobs'.

WELLS STREET facing Cole Street across the High Street junction photographed immediately before the First World War. This pair of streets was named after the Wells Cole family who owned land in the Scunthorpe area. On the left is the Trinity Wesleyan Methodist Chapel built in 1900.

A TERRACE ON THE WEST SIDE of Belgrave Square soon after the turn of the century. The row survives today although it is heavily disguised behind modern shop fronts. The gentleman in the foreground carrying a handlamp is a Great Central railwayman.

A SIMILAR VIEW to the above photograph, except that it was taken slightly farther to the east. In the background is a Primitive Methodist chapel built in 1891 that once occupied the site where Woolworths stands today.

OSWALD ROAD taken between 1910 and 1920 from a spot close to Cliff Gardens and looking towards Britannia Corner. All the elegant Edwardian villas on the right survive today, mostly unchanged externally. Fixed to the telegraph pole is an early example of electric street lighting.

TRENT VILLA, OSWALD ROAD. This house was built on the east side of the road close to Mary Street in 1906 for Mr George Drury, General Manager of the Trent Ironworks. His two young daughters can be seen standing in the porchway. It was sold in the 1930s to Pennell's Seed Merchants and has been shop premises ever since.

CROWDS GATHERED at the opening ceremony of Scunthorpe Urban District Council's Public Baths on 24 March 1932. Seated next to the microphone is Arthur Greenwood MP, a leading Labour politician, who performed the honours. He was presented with a silver key with which to open it by the building's designer, Mr W. Farrar, the Council's Engineer and Surveyor. The admission charge on opening day was 4d., which included the use of a towel.

DONCASTER ROAD looking east, at the corner of Gervase Street in the early 1960s. Little has changed since this photograph was taken, apart from the disappearance of the totem pole carrying the neon Ritz sign and even this was demolished as recently as 1990. Behind it stood the former Ritz cinema opened by David Quibell MP in 1937. Like many cinema buildings, it has experienced mixed fortunes since it ceased to show films in 1974.

THE ROYAL HOTEL, Doncaster Road, in the 1950s. It was opened on 5 April 1933 by Barnsley Breweries.

SCUNTHORPE WAR MEMORIAL pictured on its original site opposite the Old Show Ground on Doncaster Road. Very noticeable are the empty fields behind, which have since been built on. The memorial was unveiled by General Sir Ian Hamilton on Remembrance Sunday 1926 and is constructed in Aberdeen granite with concrete steps. The Scunthorpe stonemasons firm of A.E. Waters was responsible for erecting it, although the fine Sicilian marble figure of the servicemen was bought 'off the peg' from Italy, a practice which was quite common. In 1955 more lettering and a winged plaque commemorating the Royal Air Force were added and the memorial was moved to its present site outside Scunthorpe Museum.

SCUNTHORPE GENERAL HOSPITAL soon after opening when it was still surrounded by open fields. The hospital was built to commemorate servicemen from the town who died during the First World War and its first name was 'Scunthorpe War Memorial Hospital'. The foundation stone was laid by Lord Buckland of Bwelch on 13 October 1927 on land bequeathed by the Winn family. Mr Talbot Cliff formally opened the hospital on 2 December 1929.

SCUNTHORPE WAR MEMORIAL HOSPITAL NURSES' Christmas choir in full voice during the 1930s. The differences in their uniforms indicate nursing grades.

THE OUTPATIENTS DEPARTMENT, Scunthorpe War Memorial Hospital, in 1942. The ladies seated in the front row are dressed in their best clothes to see the doctor. The desk on the extreme right was used by the registrar.

A GROUP OF CHILDREN snapped by a passing photographer in the summer of 1931. The girl fifth from the left in the middle row is Linda Walker.

HENDERSON AVENUE looking towards the Circle in the 1920s with newly planted trees and recently constructed houses. The estate was the first major council housing project undertaken in Scunthorpe and was named after the then manager of Appleby-Frodingham Steelworks and energetic local councillor, James Henderson. The architect responsible for its attractive 'garden suburb' style was John Sydney Brocklesby, advised by an important figure in the field of town planning, Patrick Abercrombie.

The Changing Face of the High Street

High Street, Scunthorpe.

HIGH STREET LOOKING WEST, taken from St John's Square c. 1910. The majority of buildings in this photograph survive today. At that time most of the district's shops were situated here, as the land belonged to small landowners who were willing to sell to property developers.

THIS PHOTOGRAPH OF THE HIGH STREET was taken slightly to the west of the previous view, but at approximately the same date. On the left is the Furnace Arms, built in 1871 and the oldest public house in Scunthorpe. Opposite are Selby & Jackson's jewellers and the Union of London and Smith's bank. In a chequered career, the latter premises became Scunthorpe's Council Chamber in 1937, after being a branch of the National Provincial Bank. At the time of writing it is Scunthorpe and District Teachers' Centre.

THE NEWSAGENT'S SHOP OF JAMES WESTOBY at 13 High Street in 1909; he can be seen standing on the right. These premises date back to Scunthorpe's village days, having been erected in 1803. On sale in the window are a selection of postcards, some of which appear in this book. At this time Mr Westoby also owned a shop at 64 West Street and there was a Westoby's newsagent and tobacconist in the lower part of the High Street until the building of the shopping precinct in 1970.

BRADLEY'S DRAPERS AND OUTFITTERS at 17 High Street. The shop is chock-a-block with every type of clothing item, each with a price-tag attached.

A BUSY SCENE IN 1948. Opposite the Blue Bell (which had been rendered and whitewashed by this time) are the remains of the Empire Theatre. This was burned out in a fire in 1942 when in use as a Forces' canteen. The phalanx of workmen on bicycles, returning home from the steelworks after a shift, was once a familiar sight in the High Street.

THE BLUE BELL HOTEL festooned with decorations for the coronation of George V in 1911. Its distinguished and long-serving landlord, Robert Ingham Swaby, is in the porchway on the right.

A SAD SCENE OF DERELICTION behind one of the public bars of the Blue Bell Hotel in 1970. This was just before this famous old hotel was demolished to make way for the shopping precinct development.

A VIEW OF THE BLUE BELL in more prosperous times around the turn of the century. In the centre are the landlord and his wife, Mr and Mrs R.I. Swaby, with two of the hotel's chambermaids on their right. Waiting on the left is the Great Central Railway horse-drawn omnibus which brought patrons and their luggage from the station to the hotel. After the death of Mr Swaby in 1915, the hotel was managed by his son Arthur Swaby, before it was purchased by Shipstone's Brewery of Nottingham who owned it up to its final demise.

THE FORMAL OPENING of Scunthorpe Urban District Council's new Market Hall on 2 March 1906 by the second Baron St Oswald, Rowland Winn. The market was established under Section 166 of the 1875 Public Health Act following a poll of the ratepayers taken on 7 March 1904. The market was held every Friday and Saturday, and there was also a fortnightly cattle market. The new market replaced a smaller market which had been owned by Mr H.J. Parkinson from whom the rights and existing buildings were purchased for £5,000. Alterations including the new hall cost a further £1,500.

INTERIOR OF THE MARKET HALL soon after opening, showing Scunthorpe Confectionery Company's stall owned by Mr J. Keech. He is standing behind the counter with his arms folded.

HIGH STREET looking east towards the Manley Street junction c. 1910.

APPROXIMATELY SEVENTY YEARS LATER this photograph was taken from almost the same spot as the one above. Remarkably, the two views are almost identical. The only major change is the disappearance of the old Empire Theatre, destroyed in a fire in 1942. It was originally constructed as a Public Hall with Ben Johnson's shoe shop on the ground floor.

A SINGLE-DECKER BEDFORD OMNIBUS belonging to Enterprise and Silver Dawn Motors Ltd leaves the old bus station on the High Street for Ashby in the mid-1930s. The station consisted of three platforms and was built by the company, together with new offices and passenger facilities, in 1929.

THE OLD BUS STATION looking north towards Market Hill and Crosby Flats in the final days before demolition in 1968. It passed to Lincolnshire Road Car Co. in 1950 when they took over the Enterprise and Silver Dawn company, but by this time new facilities were badly needed. The road on the right was, in theory, a public right of way called Market Place, but it quickly became part of the bus station. Scunthorpe's present bus station was opened on 12 February 1969.

THE SECTION OF THE HIGH STREET depicted in this photograph has long been pedestrianized. The site at the junction of Cole Street and Wells Street is now occupied by British Home Stores. The building that preceded it was a splendid Wesleyan Methodist chapel called Scunthorpe Trinity Methodist Church. Its doors were opened on 5 June 1900 by Mrs Spilman of Burringham Grange who was presented with a silver key for the purpose by the Revd Isaac Newton, the first minister. It was demolished in 1959, along with the silver birch tree in the foreground, which had grown to a considerable height by then.

DEMOLITION WORK IN PROGRESS IN COLE STREET in December 1968, clearing the way for the new shopping precinct.

ONE OF SCUNTHORPE'S MOST FAMOUS RETAILERS of former years was Robinson's Ironmonger's at 83 High Street and 2 Belgrave Square, shown here in the 1920s. It was established in 1896, and as well as supplying everything from bedsteads and bedding to sewing machines and dolly tubs it also specialized in mining explosives. The latter were used in the ironstone mines where employees were expected to provide explosives as well as their own tools.

HIGH STREET looking west close to Belgrave Square after 1909.

PARKHOUSE'S FURNITURE AND CYCLE SHOP, 58 High Street, taken in 1907. This business occupied the site where Woolworths has stood since the 1930s, and was owned by Henry Brace Parkhouse. In addition to supplying new bicycles such as those displayed in the window, the shop also sold second-hand machines and accessories and undertook repairs. The posters on the wall advertise cycles manufactured by Raleigh and Rover.

HIGH STREET in the opposite direction, looking east, c. 1906. Until 1909 the portion between Belgrave Square and Britannia Corner was called 'Frodingham Road'. The sign on the left states that George Holliday (a coal dealer and wagonette proprietor) had livery stables at the rear of his premises. Scunthorpe village pump stood next to Parkhouse's shop, in the centre of the photograph.

LOOKING EAST at the junction of High Street with Frances Street in the 1920s. Frances Street leads to the entrance of Scunthorpe Cemetery and at this time its northern section was called Cemetery Road.

LOOKING WEST at the junction with Frances Street in 1933. Most of the buildings in this photograph are still standing today; their modern façades hiding the fact that they were constructed around the turn of the century.

THE OSWALD HOTEL, c. 1900, but still recognizable in this photograph as today's Tavern in the Town. Originally a private house, it was converted into a hotel in 1896 by Arthur Squire Charlesworth who extended it three years later. As a landlord he was renowned for his deafness and often made mistakes when taking customers' orders. The hotel was sold to Darley's Brewery in 1923. During the Second World War the Oswald became a popular meeting place for bomber crews from some of the big nearby airbases such as Goxhill and Kirmington.

CHILDREN AT PLAY in a very quiet High Street between Ravendale and Frances Street around 1910. At this time the houses had not yet been converted into shops.

THE BRITANNIA HOTEL has stood at the western end of the High Street since the beginning of this century, giving its name to Britannia Corner. This scene with the pony and trap dates from its earliest days when the main entrance was on the High Street rather than Frodingham Road. This change took place during alterations and extensions in 1932. The best-remembered former landlord of the hotel was Bill Pulling, licensee between 1949 and 1976.

BRITANNIA CORNER in the 1950s, with a Lincolnshire Road Car Company single-decker AEC Regal bus passing the traffic lights outside the Britannia Hotel.

Events

A SCENE FROM A GARDEN PARTY in the grounds of Wortley House in 1887. The house has been the Wortley Hotel since 1925, but in 1887 the curate at St Lawrence's Church lived there.

THE BASKET STALL at a St Lawrence's Church bazaar, c. 1910. Two of the ladies attending this amazing display of cane and basketwork are Mrs Green on the left and Emily Berridge on the right.

CELEBRATIONS IN HONOUR of the Diamond Jubilee of Queen Victoria on 22 June 1897. The decorated building is the old Conservative Club in the lower part of the High Street which still stands today. Next door was Smith & Ellison's Bank.

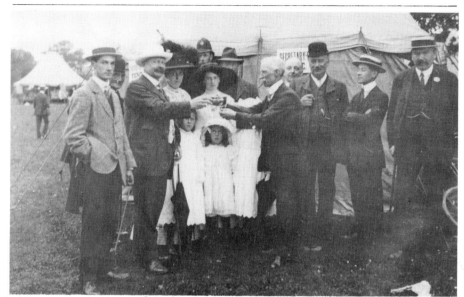

A PRIZE-GIVING CEREMONY at Scunthorpe Agricultural Show around 1910. It was first held in 1892 and, as the programme put it, was 'open to all England', with competitions for many different types of livestock, including pigeons, poultry and rabbits. Each class had its own prize cup or medal. In addition, there was also show jumping and carriage driving, and it ended with a grand firework display. Sporting events were held on a separate day.

A SCENE FROM ONE OF THE DOG DISPLAYS at Scunthorpe Agricultural Show at the Old Show Ground on 7 July 1909. There were separate classes for different breeds of dog, including sporting spaniels, pointers, curly-coated retrievers, terriers and collies.

A PANORAMIC VIEW of a post-war Scunthorpe Agricultural Show, Industrial Exhibition and Athletics Meeting. The site is now occupied by Quibell Park athletics stadium, but it was then owned by Scunthorpe Agricultural Society. The three-day event was the second largest agricultural show in Lincolnshire and cost £4,000 to organize with £2,000 offered in prizes. Today the only reminder of its former glory are the two steel 'Festival of Britain' style flagpoles on either side of the entrance.

INTERIOR OF SCUNTHORPE MARKET HALL on 22 February 1907, decorated for a by-election address by Sir Berkeley Sheffield, the Unionist candidate. In those days Scunthorpe was part of the 'Brigg Division of Lincolnshire' constituency. Sir Berkeley duly won the election held three days later, although by only a small majority over the Liberal candidate. In his campaign literature he made much of the fact that he was a Lincolnshire man.

WEDDINGS ARE ALWAYS EVENTS, and this one took place in Scunthorpe in 1916, when Miss Alice Blow was married to Mr Frederick Fletcher. Alice Blow was the daughter of the estate foreman at Brumby Hall, and Frederick Fletcher was employed at Lysaght's Steelworks.

THE CORONATION OF GEORGE V on 22 June 1911 is a contender for the title 'most photographed event in British history' and there are numerous pictures of Scunthorpe's celebrations. In this example, spectators watch a procession of schoolchildren as they parade west up the High Street. The children were one contingent of a much larger procession which set off from Church Square at 2 p.m. Later they had tea and were presented with commemorative mugs at Gurnell Street School before competing in sports events at the Old Show Field (as it was sometimes called).

A TRACTION ENGINE taken in the playground of Gurnell Street School during the same celebrations. The steam engine is performing what could be a world record for the biggest brew-up of all time! Scalding hot exhaust steam is being pumped round the canisters to brew the large amounts of tea required for the occasion.

THE FRODINGHAM PROCESSION in Cottage Beck Road to mark the coronation of George V. The decorated horse and cart is passing the New Brumby branch of the Scunthorpe Co-operative Society. Walking second from the right is Mr John Drane of Lindsey Street.

HOME STREET ON MILITARY SUNDAY, 24 April 1910. Scunthorpe Public Subscription Band leads the local Territorials back to their barracks opposite Cross Street after church parade in St John's Square.

THE APPEARANCE OF THIS PHOTOGRAPH is slightly deceptive; it suggests something more dramatic than a combined Sunday schools' trip to Cleethorpes, which took place on 17 August 1922.

HRH PRINCE GEORGE, the Duke of Kent (left), caught by the camera during a visit to Scunthorpe on 26 October 1933. He is seen here opening a new nurses' home at the War Memorial Hospital, although the main purpose of his visit was to open Scunthorpe & Frodingham Urban District Council's new section of the Doncaster–Grimsby trunk road. This is better known as Kingsway and Queensway.

Text on the float:

A COOL TIP FROM MR. THERM:
GAS NEVER LETS YOU DOWN

DON'T GO TO THE
POLE FOR IT —
MR. THERM **FW 9905**
DOES IT AT HOME!

A HOSPITAL CARNIVAL procession float waits in High Street East in the 1930s. The mobile tableau is advertising the local council gas department's refrigerators. At this time, they had a gas works in Dawes Lane, and showrooms in the old Market Hall building. Behind the float are Scunthorpe's first library, built in 1904, and the original Gurnell Street Schoolrooms erected in 1885, but long vacated when this photograph was taken.

BANDSMEN AND DECORATED BICYCLES in Frodingham Road during the Hospital Carnival procession of 1928. They are approaching Britannia Corner on their way to the Carnival Showground on Brumby Wood Lane. These annual carnivals began in 1923 and were one of the highlights of the local social scene between the wars. Their purpose was to raise money for the War Memorial Hospital.

PROCESSION OF THE CARNIVAL QUEEN at the Old Showground in 1936. The carnival queen is Enid Baxter on the left, and alongside her is her maid of honour Joyce Lingard. Although part of the Hospital Carnival, the crowning of the queen took place in a separate ceremony held at the Old Show Ground. The queen and the seven members of her retinue were chosen by a ballot of Scunthorpe Star readers.

THE ILLUMINATED OFFICES of Scunthorpe & Frodingham Urban District Council on Market Hill were an attractive sight during the Jubilee year of George V and Queen Mary in 1935. The building still remains, and one Scunthonian can vividly remember visiting it as a boy in the late 1920s. He went every week to pay part of his father's rates, which were duly entered up in a ratebook. In return, he received a green poison bottle containing disinfectant which his mother religiously poured down the drains outside their house.

CHARTER DAY, 10 October 1936. Thousands of spectators watch the Charter procession as it heads up a suitably decorated High Street on its way to the Old Showground. The procession is led by a detachment of local policemen followed by the band of His Majesty's Coldstream Guards. One surprise in this photograph is how long Marks and Spencer's have been established in High Street.

PUPILS OF SCUNTHORPE GRAMMAR SCHOOL wait in High Street East with their float before taking part in the Charter Day procession. Entitled 'Modern Scunthorpe', it was part of a combined schools' tableau of floats depicting Scunthorpe through the ages. The theme of the float just visible in front was 'The Discovery of the Ironstone by a Shooting Party'.

AN IMPORTANT MOMENT in Scunthorpe's history: Stanley George Edward Villiers, the seventeenth Earl of Derby, hands over Scunthorpe's Charter of Incorporation to Sir Berkeley Sheffield, the Charter Mayor, at a ceremony at the Old Showground. The event celebrated the town's Charter of Incorporation which was granted by King Edward VIII in recognition of the tremendous development that had taken place over the previous seventy years. Also on the podium were from the left: Councillor H. Tombs (Chairman of the Council), Mrs H. Tombs, Mr J.R. Auld (Town Clerk), The Right Reverend Nugent Hicks, Bishop of Lincoln and Councillor A.E. Dowse (Deputy Charter Mayor).

Iron and Steel

DAWES LANE taken from the tower of St John's Church c. 1900. Behind the foundry in the centre is the Trent Ironworks belching out smoke. On the right stood the former Lindsey Ironworks, disused by this date. This grimy industrial scene is only slightly relieved by the farm stackyard in the foreground.

THE FIRST OPEN-TOPPED BLAST FURNACES of the Trent Ironworks taken around 1915. These were built by George and William Dawes on land north of the railway line in 1864, and formed the first ironworks in the area. They were called the Trent Ironworks because they were originally to have been sited on the bank of the River Trent at Gunness, and the name was not forgotten. The production of iron ceased here in 1936.

FRODINGHAM IRON & STEELWORKS taken from the north around 1912 with the first mechanically-charged blast furnace to be built in Britain in the centre of the photograph. Constructed to an American design in 1905, it was nicknamed the 'Yankee' furnace. The first steel to be made in the district was cast here on 21 March 1890. Behind the peacefully grazing cows are Frodingham & Scunthorpe railway station and the Station Hotel.

A LATER VIEW of Frodingham Iron & Steelworks taken from Station Road around 1925 looking across the station yard.

A LINE-UP OF WORKMEN at the lift base of the North Lincolnshire Ironworks in 1868. They probably represent the majority of the workforce at this time. This photograph was taken by James Walsham Hall of 2 North Street, Winterton, who between 1862 and 1880 was the first professional photographer working in the area. Unfortunately few of his fine photographs were of early Scunthorpe.

APPLEBY IRONWORKS – the original four blast furnaces operating around 1900. The first of these was blown in on a site east of Scunthorpe near Santon in 1876, and because the majority of the initial capital was provided by Scotsmen it became known as the 'Scotch' company. The works was taken over by Frodingham Iron & Steel Co. in 1912.

WORKING BY HAND in the ironstone mines continued until the 1930s. In this photograph taken at that time, a sander is about to wheel a barrow load of overburden to the spoilheap at the end of the plank runway.

IRONSTONE CHUCKERS at Ashby Ville mine at around the turn of the century. Their job was to shovel the ore, which outcropped close to the surface at this time, into the railway wagons behind.

AN EARLY MECHANICAL DIGGER, possibly a converted steam railway crane, taken no later than 1920. Machines such as these were used to strip away layers of overburden. The location is the 'goosehole', Yarborough Pit, looking west.

AN APPLEBY-FRODINGHAM 'Group 50' 0–6–0 side tank engine made by Robert Stephenson & Hawthorn's Ltd accelerates out of Crosby Warren Mine with a heavy load of ironstone. It was photographed in the late 1950s and in the cab is driver Mr H. Batty.

BARROW PULLERS taken at the top of Nos. 1 and 2 furnaces, Frodingham North Ironworks, c. 1910. Their job was to hand-charge the early blast furnaces. They are from left to right: Tom Fisher (known as 'Tom Lad'), Jack Watson ('Canny Lad'), Sid Drewery and an unidentified workman. It was said that when Tom Lad and Canny Lad were charging these two furnaces they always got one or two more charges than other shifts.

A GROUP OF WORKMEN at Lysaght's Normanby Park steelworks. The men have been unloading wagons under the watchful eye of the foreman standing on the right. Blast furnaces are to the left, with the melting shop beyond.

MISS RENEE KILBY, daughter of General Manager Joe Kilby, lights a new blast furnace at Redbourn Ironworks in May 1939. This furnace gave an output of 1,500 tons of iron a week, and provided jobs for an extra fifty men.

PIG CASTING BY HAND at Redbourn Ironworks in July 1946. The molten iron is being run off into pig beds moulded in sand.

THE ORIGINAL CAPTION on this photograph reads, 'Distribution of beef and bread during strike 13–5–09 given by Mr S. Charlesworth'. It was taken in Scunthorpe High Street close to the Oswald Hotel of which Arthur Squire Charlesworth was the landlord. The strike of 1909 was over union recognition and a bonus disagreement and it was finally resolved after four weeks with the mediation of the local MP, Sir Berkeley Sheffield. Squire Charlesworth had himself worked in the iron and steel industry, and 'Squire' was not a nickname, but his real name.

DELIVERY WAGON BELONGING to John Lysaght's Joint Works Committee Coal Club, taken around 1930. The club was a non-profit making organization formed in 1926 with the aim of supplying its members with cheaper coal and a better delivery service than that obtainable from local coal merchants. A rota system was operated to ensure deliveries to members' homes on approximately the same day of each month.

A GANG OF LYSAGHT'S RAILWAYMEN taken in front of one of the company's steam locomotives in 1931. When it opened in 1912, Lysaght's was the last new steelworks to be built in Scunthorpe. It was connected to the main railway network via Dragonby sidings, and like the other major works it also maintained its own internal rail network.

JOHN LYSAGHT'S NORMANBY PARK STEELWORKS BRASS BAND, c. 1935.

THE STATION HOTEL taken in the 1950s showing just how close it once stood to Frodingham Ironworks. At one time it was a lunchtime meeting place for local businessmen as well as being the first port of call on the way home for many a thirsty steelworker. Built in 1888, the hotel was demolished exactly seventy years later to make way for road widening.

A GAME OF DOMINOES and a pint inside the old Station Hotel in the 1950s. In its heyday this was the foremost steelworkers' public house in Scunthorpe; somewhere to congregate after work and discuss the day's events. It also opened early in the morning so that workmen finishing a shift could obtain liquid refreshment before breakfast.

MECHANICAL CHARGING of an open-hearth steel furnace at Redbourn Melting Shop in June 1947. The charging machine in the photograph has a long arm which extended through the door of the furnaces, dropping in the charge of lime or scrap.

People and Personalities

A LATE VICTORIAN STUDIO PORTRAIT of Uriah Long, the Scunthorpe miller, and his wife, who were married in 1855. Three years later he built Scunthorpe windmill and continued to operate it until 1920.

A CARTE-DE-VISITE PHOTOGRAPH of Henry Healey (1784–1868). A member of a well-known local landowning family, he was the first owner of Ashby Decoy, constructed in 1833. Decoys were a means of trapping wild duck, then an important food source. He was born in High Risby and died in Scarborough where this portrait was taken.

SCUNTHORPE SUB-POSTMASTER THOMAS NAINBY taken around 1890 complete with a 'Premier' safety bicycle (at this time postmen received an allowance for using their own machines). Apart from the cap, however, he is wearing fashionable cycling clothes rather than a uniform. Mr Nainby also ran a draper's shop. The service he operated was very efficient, with letters delivered at 11.50 a.m. and 6.10 p.m.

HENRY BRACE PARKHOUSE (1859–1939), a local steel pioneer. He came to Scunthorpe in 1890 to work with Maximilian Mannaberg on the first steel-making furnaces at Frodingham Ironworks. He was also a local councillor, and owned a furniture and cycle shop in the High Street. In later years he worked abroad, and is reputed to have been the first man to make steel in Spain.

MRS ARTHUR HOWDEN feeds a donkey in the garden of Vicarage Cottage, Frodingham. Her husband ran a private school in Frodingham and was also the census enumerator for the district. The boy is Arthur Howden Swaby, grandson of R.I. Swaby.

A ST JOHN'S CHURCH women's group, c. 1910. Among those present are back row, left to right: Lena Stubbins, Miss Leggard, Ethel Read, Mrs Hornsby, Jessie Berridge; third row: Rose Skelton, Mrs D. Dixon, Patty Robson, Emily Berridge, Maria Baratt; second row: Linda Snowden, Miss Bainton, Amy Bainton, Ethel Leake; front row: Mrs Leake, Mrs Robson, Miss Ashdown, Miss Brown.

THE SMARTLY ATTIRED EDWARDIAN GENTLEMAN is Arthur Squire Charlesworth (1848–1931), seen here holding his grandson Arthur. After moving from Cleckheaton to Scunthorpe in 1894, he worked for a short time as a foreman boilersmith at Frodingham Iron & Steelworks before opening the Oswald Hotel and becoming a property developer.

ROBERT INGHAM SWABY (1832–1915) was well known as the landlord of the Blue Bell Hotel between 1864 and his death. Any suggestion that he and Squire Charlesworth were rivals is refuted by his being the best man at the latter's second wedding.

R.I. SWABY is also seen here, in one of the first motor cars to visit Scunthorpe, in about 1908. The driver is Mr Hanley.

THIS IS MR J.G. GRAHAM, baker, pastrycook and confectioner, proudly displaying the results of his work in about 1905. He made wedding and birthday cakes to order from his 'hygienic bakery' at 21 West Street, as well as more everyday products such as freshly baked plain and brown bread, milk cakes, tea cakes and scones.

THESE ELEGANTLY DRESSED EDWARDIAN LADIES outside Oswald Farm are, from left to right: Mrs A. Swaby, Mrs W. Woodley and Mrs L.J. Beardsley.

PC JOSHUA SAUNBY photographed outside the old courthouse building. He joined the Scunthorpe Division of the Lincolnshire Constabulary in 1913.

A MIXED INFANTS' CLASS PHOTOGRAPH taken outside Frodingham School around 1912. The teachers are Miss Heseltine on the left and Miss Moorman on the right. Incredibly 700 pupils were attending this relatively small school at this time and there were 21 teachers.

A GROUP OF TRAINEE TEACHERS in 1922 outside Cole Street Higher Elementary School and Pupil Teachers' Centre, which is now an annexe of the North Lindsey Technical College. This class was the last to take the preliminary examination for the teacher's certificate. Among those present are back row, left to right: E. Hassall, I. Jones, E. Holmes, D. Blyth, B. Sumpter, D. Wall, D. Watkinson; middle row: H. McLaughlin, M. Haith, D. Marshall, L. Edwards; front row: C. Hancock, W. Bramley, H. Roberts.

THE STAFF OF SCUNTHORPE GRAMMAR SCHOOL in 1940. Mr W.A. Taylor, the long-serving headmaster in the centre of the front row, retired just two years after this photograph was taken.

A ST JOHN'S CHURCH STAFF PHOTOGRAPH dating from early 1911. The clergy are, from left to right: Revd E. Comer (Assistant Curate), Revd A.E.G. Smith (Senior Curate), Revd T. Boughton (Vicar) and Revd B.G. Parsons (Assistant Curate). The lay members seated are: Mr Nelson (a Navvy Missioner), Miss Ashdown (daughter of the previous vicar) and Mr A. Garlick (Lay Reader and Parish Secretary). Mr Nelson had recently arrived in Scunthorpe to work with the 500 or so men employed constructing Lysaght's Steelworks, and the photograph was taken to give to the Revd Smith as a leaving present. Postcard copies could be obtained from Mr Garlick, price 2d.

THESE FOUR GENTLEMEN are pictured in the grounds of a house on Oswald Road, around 1930. They are wearing fashionable formal daywear of the period, and are, from left to right: S. Fraser, J. Bannister, A. Walker and C. Crooke.

IT WOULD BE POSSIBLE TO WRITE A BOOK about the man on the right of this photograph, Reginald Anthony Colmer Symes (1877–1933), and in fact one already has been. Pictured here with his wife Ethel, he has been described as 'one of Scunthorpe's greatest citizens'. 'Reggie' was a successful solicitor, and of the many contribution he made to the life of the town in the early decades of this century, the formation of the Keenites Society is his most famous. This was a Christian boys' club, which grew out of number of Bible classes held under his leadership. Their headquarters was the 'Keenhouse', situated behind his offices in High Street.

THE COUNT MEETS THE MAYOR. Legendary American bandleader William Basie chats to the Mayor of Scunthorpe, Councillor Gerald McQuade JP in October 1957. This was during a visit to celebrate the twenty-first anniversary of the granting of Scunthorpe's Borough Charter, when the Count Basie Orchestra played two concerts at the Pavilion Cinema. The band was at the height of its powers, and featured the powerful lead vocals of Big Joe Williams. Gerry McQuade was then the town's youngest Mayor, and with him in the photograph is his consort Mrs McQuade.

A WELL-KNOWN FIGURE who is remembered by many Scunthonians, to whom he taught road safety, is PC Reginald Wood BEM. Here he demonstrates the finer points of bicycle maintenance to a group of schoolchildren at the former model traffic area in Laneham Street in the mid-1960s. It was opened by HM The Queen on 27 June 1958, and no less than 16,000 children were trained there by PC Wood up to 1974.

Scunthorpe at Work

THE SCUNTHORPE FIRM OF JOHNSON CYCLES manufactured bicycles and motorcycles for a relatively short period between 1892 and 1905. The owner was George James Bell Johnson who originally had premises in High Street but later moved to Trafford, naming his new factory the Beeston Cycle and Motor Works which is shown here. Lined up outside are examples of the firm's products. After 1905 the building became St John's Parish Church Hall.

SYDNEY DUDLEY COLLEY on an early type of moped, manufactured by Johnson Cycles. The Colley family provided capital for the enterprise, and the date is soon after the turn of the century. Apart from the motoring cap Sydney is dressed in typical Edwardian cycling costume.

COTTO PRODUCTS LTD trade stand taken in the 1930s, location not known. This Scunthorpe firm was well known throughout the country for their hand-operated washing machines and later for their electric clothes-driers. At one time their name rivalled other national brands such as Ewbank, Hotpoint and Thor; in 1936, they could advertise that 'Cotto does the nation's washing'. On display are examples of their 'standard' and 'jean de luxe' washers and one of their early gas washers.

THIS POSTCARD of housebuilders taken in 1935 depicts a typical Scunthorpe scene between the wars. They have just finished constructing the roof. A rapidly rising population led to the building of 5,717 private and 1,188 council houses during that period.

THE ENTIRE COMPLEMENT OF Scunthorpe Divisional Police Force photographed outside the old courthouse and police station buildings in Station Road. Seated in the centre of the front row is Superintendent Melbourn Holmes with, on his left and right, Sergeant Hill and Inspector Metcalfe respectively. Third from the left is Sergeant Dawson and on his right, at the end of the front row, is Police Constable Saunby. Inspector Holmes was stationed in various other parts of Lincolnshire and rose from the ranks to become superintendent of the Scunthorpe Division in 1901. He retired in 1921 and this is possibly his retirement photograph.

SCUNTHORPE FIRE BRIGADE testing their first fire engine. It is a horse-drawn Greenwich Gem steamer, which was presented to the brigade by Sir Berkeley Sheffield in November 1908. Third from the right in this photograph, taken soon afterwards, is C.P. Shepherd, who was a 'call boy'. His job was to take messages to and from the fire station and from fires. The engine was very efficient for its day, having a capacity of 250 to 350 gallons a minute and being able to throw a jet of water to a height of 150 ft.

THE CONSTRUCTION OF THE HOSE TOWER, during the building of Scunthorpe's original fire station in Cole Street, taken in 1909. The tower was fitted with a lantern and bell and equipped with blocks and pulleys for drawing up the hoses for drying.

SCUNTHORPE FIRE BRIGADE OFFICERS taken outside the entrace to the Cole Street Fire Station in 1928. In the centre is the Captain of the Fire Brigade, Thomas Sudlow, with from left to right, Firemen: Twivey, Begg, J. Harsley, Sanderson, H. Proundlove and H. Leaning. The station was built by Scunthorpe Urban District Council on a site costing £800 at the junction with Mary Street. It was in use for fifty-nine years until the present station in Laneham Street was opened in 1963. Demolition finally took place in 1976.

THE AFTERMATH OF THE FIRE at Frodingham Chemical Works which took place on 17 September 1906. It destroyed much of the factory which was situated on Brigg Road close to Frodingham Iron & Steel Works. The fire was the main reason for the formation of a local fire brigade, as extinguishers were the only fire-fighting appliances available in Scunthorpe at the time and the blaze had to be left to burn itself out.

A GROUP OF RAILWAY STAFF taken on the down platform of Frodingham & Scunthorpe station during the First World War. The gable end of the old courthouse building can be seen on the extreme right of the photograph. The preponderance of women, including shunting staff, shows the extent to which they were recruited to fill jobs vacated by men serving at the Front. The figure in the centre in the straw hat is the yard-master Charlie Oates.

RAILWAYMEN AND WOMEN taken outside one of the signal boxes at Normanby Park Sidings on the North Lindsey Light Railway during the First World War. These sidings acted as a marshalling yard for traffic into and out of Lysaght's Steelworks. On the right is the station-master, Mr G.W. Mawson.

SPILMAN'S MONUMENTAL MASON'S YARD on Station Road, taken immediately after the turn of the century from an upper storey window of the Constitutional Club opposite. The firm started up here in the late 1870s but later moved to Chapel Street.

MEMBERS OF THE STAFF of Fred Cowham's hairdressing saloons taken outside the shop around 1900. At this time his address was 4 Frodingham Road, but it later became 92 High Street when the name of the Street was changed in 1909. In those days there were just five barbers' shops in the area, serving a population of around 10,000 people. One description of the haircuts of the day was 'all off except the eyebrows and no fringe'.

SCUNTHORPE & DISTRICT STEAM LAUNDRY'S first delivery vehicle in the early 1920s. In the cab of the Model T Ford van is Miss Austin at the wheel, with Miss Bradley on her right. The laundry was established in 1907 and for many years was in business in Clayfield Road (renamed Doncaster Road in 1923). When this photograph was taken, it also had a receiving office at 123 High Street and agents in surrounding villages.

TWO SHOPS ON MARKET HILL taken after the turn of the century. They are Edward Ainger's furniture shop at 3 Market Hill and John William Gunn's ironmonger's next door. At this time the two shops together could supply everything a young couple might need to set up home.

THE STAFF AND SHOP WINDOW of Long's butchers shop in the 1930s. It once traded at 57 High Street, between Manley Street and Cole Street. Note the wicker-basketed carrier bicycles held by the two butcher's boys.

THE OPEN SHOP FRONTAGE of the Grimsby Fish Supply Company at 75 High Street in a fascinating photograph taken at Christmas-time around 1920. Marks and Spencer's occupy this site today. Rather confusingly, in view of its name, it advertised as being the 'leading firm in town for game, poultry, fish, fruit, bouquets etc'. The owner, Mr Arthur Laughton, is standing on the left and behind him a hand-written sign offers 'compliments of the season to all' and reminds customers 'not to forget their Xmas cheer'. On the right is his brother-in-law, William Oxley, in front of a poster advertising the Palace Theatre in Cole Street.

DINES LTD, 110 SCUNTHORPE HIGH STREET, taken in the 1920s, at a time of the day when it was obviously open. This pleasant fish and chip restaurant stood on the north side of High Street between Wells Street and Gilliat Street and there was a dance floor upstairs for parties and receptions. An attractive feature is the lattice windows with their bull's-eye glass panes.

THE STAFF OF DINES'S FISH RESTAURANT, on the pavement outside in 1926. The gentleman in the suit on the left was the manager Jess Wade and on the right is the fish-buyer, Ted Marris. The chicly dressed young lady in the middle of the front row was the resident pianist.

A DELIVERY LORRY IN THE HIGH STREET, belonging to George Howson, a fish and fruit merchant. The date is soon after the First World War, and the figure in the centre, wearing a cap, is Tommy Hall.

WORKMEN AND A STEAMROLLER belonging to Scunthorpe & Frodingham Urban District Council, c. 1930.

SCUNTHORPE'S FIRST TAXI, owned by Henry Skelton, captured in the early 1920s. The vehicle is a touring version of the Model T Ford.

THE CREW OF a Scunthorpe & Frodingham Urban District Council Highways Department steam lorry in East Common Lane in 1921.

A GREAT CENTRAL RAILWAY HORSE-DRAWN PARCELS VAN outside Frodingham & Scunthorpe station around 1906. The young man on the right is Mr W. Milner. At this time the various railway companies employed enormous numbers of horses for delivery work.

A LINE-UP OF THE DRIVERS AND VEHICLES of the Progressive Motor Omnibus Service. This company came to Scunthorpe in 1922 and by 1925 had established offices in Grosvenor Street, only to merge with Enterprise and Silver Dawn Motors Ltd in the same year. During this short period the company concentrated on services between Scunthorpe and the surrounding villages, as can be seen from the destination boards of the Straker Squire double-deckers. The location is almost certainly the foot of newly constructed Doncaster Road.

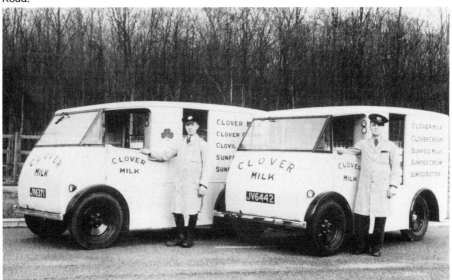

CLOVER MILK DELIVERY VANS in the 1950s when they advertised that 'every bottle of Clover milk stands for supreme purity and richness of flavour'. Their dairy was in Parkinson Avenue.

Scunthorpe at War

THE 'K' FRODINGHAM COMPANY, of the Lincolnshire Territorials, at their annual camp around 1890. The bearded gentleman in the centre is the Revd E.M. Weigall, Chaplain of the Lincolnshire Regiment and also Vicar of Frodingham (1859–1908). When he died in 1908 he was buried with full military honours.

THE FIRST SCUNTHORPE BOER WAR VOLUNTEERS in 1899. On the right of the middle row is Private J.W. Drury.

CROWDS GATHERED IN STATION ROAD to greet the return of the volunteers from the Boer War in 1901. They were driven in the wagonette to St John's Church, where a service of thanksgiving was held. After the service the procession was re-formed and it paraded around Scunthorpe, which was decorated for the occasion. An estimated 10,000 people turned out to welcome them home.

WILLIAM WOODLEY in uniform as Drum Major of the 5th Battalion of the Lincolnshire Regiment during the First World War. He was perhaps better known as 'King Bill', the proprietor of the Queen Hotel in New Frodingham and later of the Sheffield Arms in Grimsby.

A POIGNANT PHOTOGRAPH of First World War volunteers mobilized on Frodingham & Scunthorpe station in 1914. On the left is Drum Major William Woodley from the previous photograph.

WATCHED BY A CROWD OF ONLOOKERS, Frodingham Territorials wait for the train to Grimsby en route for France during the first year of the First World War.

THIS IS PRIVATE JOHN 'JACK' CUNNINGHAM VC, who was born in Scunthorpe in 1897. He won a Victoria Cross during the Battle of the Somme while serving as a bomber in the East Yorkshire Regiment. This gallant soldier survived the war but died aged 43 in Hull, where he had lived for most of his life.

REGIMENTAL SERGEANT MAJOR JOHN ATTON of the Lincolnshire Regiment at camp, looking every inch the smartly turned out warrant officer. Before the First World War, he was the Drill Instructor to 'G' Company of the 5th Battalion of the Lincolnshire Regiment whose Drill Hall was at 19 Home Street, Scunthorpe.

FIRST ROUTE MARCH SCUNTHORPE V.T.C. 21-3-1915.
Photo By H. Skelton Scunthorpe

SCUNTHORPE VOLUNTEER TRAINING COMPANY taken on 21 March 1915 outside the Sheffield Arms in Burton Stather on their first route march. These men formed part of the 'New Army' that fought on the Somme.

THIS PHOTOGRAPH WAS TAKEN at the lower end of the High Street during the visit of a First World War tank. The purpose was to promote War Bonds and after the end of hostilities the tank, nicknamed 'Egbert', was displayed for some years in front of the east end of St John's Church.

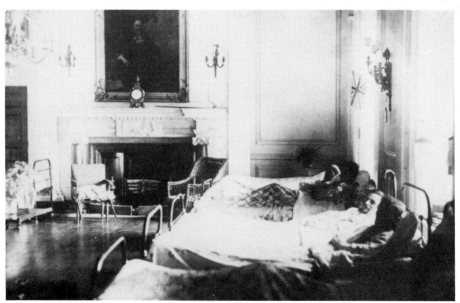

DURING THE FIRST WORLD WAR Normanby Hall was appropriated for use as a military hospital. Here wounded soldiers convalesce in a ward converted from one of the ground floor rooms.

A SCENE ALL TOO FAMILIAR on the Home Front during the Second World War; a ration queue waits outside Hunting's tobacconists on the High Street for its allocation of sweets and tobacco. Its owner, Lt.-Col. Norman Hunting, commanded Scunthorpe Home Guard. The shop is still there today.

SCUNTHORPE WAS VISITED BY CLEMENT ATTLEE, Lord Privy Seal in the War Cabinet, on 21 September 1940. Here he watches casting at Redbourn Iron & Steelworks through protective spectacles. On his left are Joe Kilby, the Works Manager, Councillor G.H. Spavin, the Mayor, and Dr Russell Stanforth. The visit was organized partly to compensate for the exclusion of Redbourn Works from a Royal visit which took place a month previously.

SALVAGE FORMED AN IMPORTANT PART of the war effort. Here, a work party organized by Bottesford & Yaddlethorpe Women's Institute stands beside a pile of scrap in Yaddlethorpe High Street. The adults are, left to right: Mrs Gilliat, Mrs Dexter, Mrs Bristow, Mrs Haig, Mrs Blackbourne, Mrs Martin and an unidentified gentleman. The children are, left to right: Phyllis Robinson, G. Hindley and Brian Robinson.

OFFICERS OF THE LOCAL HOME GUARD take a break during manoeuvres. On the left is Scunthorpe Section Commander Lt.-Col. Norman Hunting enjoying the contents of his mess tin.

THE FINAL STANDING-DOWN PARADE of Scunthorpe Home Guard on a grey December day in 1944. The men are passing a civic group containing the Mayor and Aldermen standing outside the Public Baths on Doncaster Road.

SCUNTHORPE AUXILIARY FIRE SERVICE on parade in Oswald Road.

FORE SECTION OF A UTILITY SHIP made by Orthostyle, the Scunthorpe firm of constructional engineers. During the war, they were engaged in specialized production work, most notably for the D-day PLUTO project (Pipe Line Under The Ocean). They also made landing craft and 70 ft prefabricated Utility ships such as the one pictured here. Sections of these tugs were prepared at their works for assembly at shipyards.

RESIDENTS CROWD CLIFF STREET, New Frodingham, on 9 May 1945 during VE Day celebrations to mark the end of the Second World War in Europe.

SMITH STREET AND BERKELEY STREET VE Day celebrations on the same day; the scene is set for the children's party. Street parties were prepared some time in advance, and after services of thanksgiving, festivities went on into the small hours of the next morning. At 11 p.m. a large bonfire, originally designed to mislead enemy aircraft, was lit at Appleby-Frodingham Steelworks.

Sport and Leisure

SMITH & WARREN'S FAIR in the Old Stackyard in 1915. The site is roughly where Scunthorpe's open market is today, and was originally the rear of a farm on the High Street owned by Edward Dore. Some of the first films to be seen in Scunthorpe were shown at these fairs as side-show attractions known as 'Bioscopes'.

COLE STREET in the 1920s with the Palace Theatre on the right. The building has now been converted into a supermarket, but between 1912 and 1954 it was a flourishing theatre presenting a wide range of travelling repertory companies and variety acts. For example, during the week commencing 4 June 1928 the theatre had for a short season Mrs Ennis Lawson and her 'renowned repertory company of famous players', billed as 'undoubtedly the best repertory touring'. Their programme consisted of *French Leave*, 'the sparkling comedy' on Monday and Tuesday, *Outward Bound*, 'the striking and original play' on Wednesday and Thursday, followed by *Camille* on Friday and *Trilby* on Saturday. Renamed the Savoy in 1938, the theatre became the Essoldo Cinema sixteen years later, but still continued to stage the occasional pantomime.

A SCUNTHORPE OPERATIC SOCIETY publicity photograph for a production of *HMS Pinafore* taken on the stage of the old Public Hall in 1910. The characters are Little Buttercup played by Mrs F. Geary, and Captain Corcoran played by Mr J. Bickerton. The opera ran for five nights and was the society's second production (it having been formed a year earlier). Strangely, this is the only time in the society's distinguished history that this Gilbert & Sullivan opera has been performed.

AN EARLY AMATEUR THEATRICAL GROUP taken outside Frodingham School some time after the turn of the century. The lady seated is Mrs Beardsley, the headmistress of the infants' section of the school, and the group was drawn from the congregation of St Lawrence's Church.

A SCENE FROM APPLEBY-FRODINGHAM THEATRICAL SOCIETY'S 1959 production of *The Lovebirds* by Basil Thomas. This was one of the first plays to be staged at Scunthorpe's new Civic Theatre, which opened in May 1958. The society, which has been one of the mainstays of Scunthorpe's long and distinguished amateur dramatic tradition, was formed in the typing pool of Appleby-Frodingham Steel Co. on 29 November 1951. Among the cast on stage are Hilda Donald, Harry Botton, Greta Belton, Mary Seamer and Arthur Hill.

SANTON ATHLETIC FC was a successful local football team and Lindsey League champions in the 1922/3 season. The line-up then was back row, left to right: -?-, Johnny Hanslow, Lew Clarke, Roy King, Jack Wilks (trainer); middle row: Marsh Jackson, 'Tig' Clarke, -?-, Joe Ridgely; front row: Albert Robinson, Fred King, Albert Bowers, Larry Bowers, Fred Hodson.

Scunthorpe United Football Club, Season 1904-5.

Winners of Frodingham Charity Cup, Winterton Charity Cup and
North Lindsey League.

SCUNTHORPE UNITED FC, season 1904/5. At this early date, the club was still an amateur team playing in the North Lindsey League. Only when they amalgamated with another local side, Lindsey United, in 1910, did they turn professional, joining the Midland League two years later. In 1904 United were already playing at the Old Show Ground.

SCUNTHORPE BOROUGH MAYOR, Councillor G. McQuade JP, presents Scunthorpe United captain Frank Marshall with the 'Sunday People Giant Killers Cup' at a home game at the Old Show Ground in 1958. This was awarded for their achievement in reaching the fifth round of the FA Cup, which included a 3–1 away victory over First Division Newcastle United. It was also the season United gained promotion to the Second Division of the Football League by winning the Third Division North Championship.

SCUNTHORPE UNITED TEAM AND OFFICIALS pictured in the January snow of 1954 before travelling to a fourth round FA Cup replay against First Division Portsmouth. The game ended in a two–all draw after extra time, but unfortunately United lost the replay held at Arsenal's Highbury Stadium in North London. This was only their fourth season in the Football League which they had joined in 1950. The popularity of post-war soccer can be gauged from the fact that a total of 78,722 spectators watched the three games. A redoubtable figure on the extreme right of this photograph is Harry Alcock. He was the club secretary for forty years between 1915 and 1955. Also of interest is the Lincolnshire Road Car Company luxury Bedford coach hired for the occasion.

CLOSE FIELDERS surround a batsman during a Minor Counties cricket match involving Lincolnshire at Brumby Hall in the late 1950s. The pitch was regarded as the best in the old county, and it was the venue of an annual cricket festival.

SCUNTHORPE GOLF CLUB'S putting green and club house in 1936. The nine-hole course opened without ceremony on 11 April of that year, on land that had previously been part of Ashby Decoy Farm. It was the brainchild of Mr V. Jenkins and Mr F. Gladwin who became the club's first captain and club secretary respectively. The club house was converted from what was described as a 'picturesque' farm cottage.

PARTICIPANTS IN A FRIENDLY SHOOTING MATCH organized by Scunthorpe & District Rifle Club on 27 June 1915. The contest was between teams organized by Dr Behrendt and Mr H. Kiddle, the latter's team winning by 46 points.

FISHING CLUB PRESENTATION outside the Reform Club in Cross Street in 1921. Only a few trophies were presented to the successful anglers, instead more useful items such as crockery, furniture and bedding were awarded.

RENOWNED SCUNTHORPE CYCLIST Albert 'Lal' White at a grass-track meeting in the 1920s. Standing behind him is his brother, Charlie White, who was also a successful rider. Not only was Lal one of Scunthorpe's greatest sportsmen, he was also one of Britain's finest cyclists, winning thirteen National Championships in different events. He also represented Britain on no fewer than six occasions in Olympic events and won a silver medal in Paris in 1924. Of his other claims to fame, he also featured on a ci- garette card in the Gallagher series 'British champions' of 1923.

SCUNTHORPE ROLLER HOCKEY TEAM at the Geisha Roller Skating Rink in around 1909. Between 1908 and 1910 a roller-skating craze swept the country, resulting in purpose-built roller-skating rinks springing up in towns like Scunthorpe. One aspect of the craze was roller hockey, and teams such as this one competed against opponents from other towns. They are, from left to right, standing: T. Danson, H. Spavin, ? Rylatt, F.H.W. Atkinson (Manager); seated: J. Spavin, F. Spavin, J. Barley. Like all crazes it was short-lived, and the roller-skating rink, which had been built on open land on Clayfield Road in 1909, was converted into the Pavilion Cinema four years later.

THE PAVILION CINEMA on Doncaster Road at the corner of Gervase Street in the 1950s. The name of the cinema lives on in Pavilion Row, the line of shops that now occupies the site. This was the largest of Scunthorpe's eight cinemas, with seating for 1,371 patrons, and its nickname 'the Rink', came from its use as a roller-skating rink. Albert 'Tickteen' Roebuck is remembered as a local character who worked there for over thirty years as boilerman, caretaker and usher.

WILF BILSON'S ORCHESTRA captured on the stage of the Pavilion Cinema in 1926. This remarkably large ensemble would accompany silent pictures from scores which were sent in advance of the film. Wilf, a violinist, is seated cross-legged in the centre of the photograph. For a brief period in the 1920s he also ran orchestras at the Palace Variety Theatre, and the Majestic and the Royal cinemas. With the coming of the 'talkies' in 1929, however, this orchestra like most of the others was replaced by a cinema organ.

SCUNTHORPE & DISTRICT TOTAL ABSTINENCE PRIZE BRASS BAND taken outside Frodingham Vicarage (now the Museum) in 1907. They were the winners of two first prizes at Winterton on 22 June of that year. They are, back row, left to right: T.B. Pickup (correspondence secretary), J.W. Houlden (committee), E. Apperton (committee), H. Lee, T. Drummond, B. Arrand; second row: W. Dalton, G. Wright, A. Harrison, E. Rily, C. Burkill, H. Langton, G. King; third row: C. Barr, T. Spriggs, H. Smelt, S. Arrand, G. Harrison, F. Wiseman, J. Smith, W. Arrand (chairman of committee); front row: J.W. Maw, C.R. Smelt, T.C. Sharp (financial secretary), D. Leeman (bandmaster), G. Watson, H. Bones, E. Headland, ? McConell, R.J. Theaker.

A DANCE BAND taken at the Berkeley Hotel on 28 February 1947 by Scunthorpe photographer Alec N. Hainsworth. The band is thought to be a semi-professional outfit from Doncaster called 'Buller's Band', and not one of the popular Scunthorpe bands such as the Les Markham Band or the Arcadians. There is no bass player in the line-up, as in those days a double bass was something of a luxury, due to transport problems.

A HIGHFIELD HOUSE PIGEON FLYING CLUB official checks timers during the 1950s. The secretary of the club at this time was Mr H. Proudlove.

A CHILDREN'S CHRISTMAS PARTY in progress at the Lysaght's Institute in October 1965. The group consists of children of the company's Nettleton Mines employees. Known as the 'Foxhills Club', the institute was opened on 12 November 1956 by Lysaght's Works General Manager, Sir Charles Bruce-Gardner. This was the last time their party was held there, as the following year it was transferred to a new club house at Nettleton.

A CROWDED SCUNTHORPE PUBLIC SWIMMING BATHS in 1950. This pool was originally built as an adults only senior baths, and became known as the 'Big Baths'. During the winter months it was covered over with a polished maple floor and used for dancing, a practice which only ceased with the opening of the Leisure Centre in 1983. Younger swimmers often took great delight in climbing on to the balcony and 'bombing' the water below, an activity much frowned upon by the attendants!

A ST JOHN'S CHURCH PICNIC OUTING to Burton Hills, a local beauty spot, on a Whit Monday around 1908. The mixed cycle company is about to set off from the lower part of the High Street, and other members travelled by wagonette.

ACKNOWLEDGEMENTS

The majority of photographs in this book are from the collections of Scunthorpe Museum and Art Gallery and thanks are therefore due to the kindness of the many individuals who have donated photographs over the years.

I would like to thank the following for their generous help: John Baker, Peter Batty, Sue Broadbent, Susan Hopkinson, Kevin Leahy, Stanley Melton, Keith Miller, Grace Parrott, Carol Rees, Jack Sergeant, Yvette Staelens, Muriel Steeper, James Taylor, the staff of Scunthorpe Central Library Reference Section, Janet Tierney, Reginald Wood.